Praise for *Girls Gone Wise ... in a World Gone Wild*

Mary Kassian speaks with rare insight, clarity, directness, and grace as she challenges the prevailing winds of our culture. She paints portraits of two contrasting kinds of women and sets forth a vision that calls women out of their dysfunction, pain, and deception, to walk in the light of God's redeeming truth and grace. This book is extremely important, timely, and needed—I cannot think of any category of women (or men, for that matter) who could not benefit greatly from reading it and grappling with these critical issues. A "must-read" for women who desire to honor God with their lives and to influence others to do the same.

NANCY LEIGH DEMOSS, author, host of Revive Our Hearts radio

This is a wonderful book with amazing insight into the hearts of women (and men!) who feel pressured by today's "wild" culture—and also deep, spiritual insight into the Bible's wisdom regarding the beauty of true womanhood as God created it to be.

WAYNE GRUDEM, PHD, research professor of Theology and Biblical Studies, Phoenix Seminary, Phoenix, Arizona

Mary Kassian has done it again. With aplomb, grace, and wisdom, she sets the right course through some of the most treacherous and dangerous issues of our day. With just the right balance of truth and understanding, Mary calls girls and young women to a bold, strong, and biblical model of true womanhood—an understanding that honors God and shows the world a counterrevolutionary model of genuine womanhood. When Mary Kassian writes a book, women can count on sound advice and biblical wisdom from a gracious friend.

R. ALBERT MOHLER JR., president, The Southern Baptist Theological Seminary

So much of life is broken because our standards come from the world rather than from the precepts of God's Word. Our young people are living in the rubble of destruction and need rescuing from the earthquake of the consequences of not building their lives on truth. Mary's book *Girls Gone Wise . . . in a World Gone Wild* is a needed book for our times. May it grab our attention and drive us to His Word where Mary will take us.

KAY ARTHUR, CEO and cofounder Precept Ministries International, author of *The Truth about Sex: What the World Won't Tell You and What God Wants You To Know,* and *Return to the Garden: Embracing God's Design for Sexuality*

Girls today are growing up in a culture where "bad" has become the new "good." The glamorization of bad behavior among young women has become the new norm, and left in its wake a tremendous amount of fallout and misery. Mary has penned a handbook for reversing the tide of the girls-gone-wild trend and replacing it with a new rank of girls-gone-wise. I can't wait to recommend this book!

VICKI COURTNEY, bestselling author of *Your Girl* and *5 Conversations You Must Have With Your Daughter*

Many women today are eager for mentors. While a book is never a substitute for a real, live mentor, this one does connect women everywhere to the wise counsel of Mary Kassian. And we should heed her winsome, culturally relevant, and biblically sound words in *Girls Gone Wise*. This book provides an accurate gauge of the current feminine perspective in Western culture and contrasts it with the eternal wisdom found in Scripture. Easy-to-read, humble, humorous, and thoroughly sound, *Girls Gone Wise* is a book both long-time believers and new converts will benefit from reading. Highly recommended!

CAROLYN MCCULLEY, author, *Radical Womanhood: Feminine Faith in a Feminist World*

This book sounds a clear and much-needed message regarding the ethics of biblical womanhood. Mary Kassian's energy and passion make it a readable book. Her eye-opening contrast between the wise and the wild make it a convicting book. Her faithfulness to Scripture makes it a compelling book.

SUSAN HUNT, author, consultant for women's ministries for the Presbyterian Church in America

Girl's Gone Wise is a crucial message for such a time as this. In a culture where true femininity is in danger of extinction, young women are desperate to catch a vision for God's pattern. Mary Kassian's relevant, practical, and biblically based insights give today's young women a clear, inspiring blueprint for the only version of womanhood that truly fulfills—God's version.

ERIC AND LESLIE LUDY, bestselling authors of *When God Writes Your Love Story*

Mary Kassian will help you navigate the overexposure we experience every day to messages that call us to be anything but what God created us to be as women. Her message will make you wise to that, and hungry to be what God intended. I think this would be a great book for moms to read with their teen girls. Though Mary navigates critical worldview issues and strong theology, she does it with a conversational and contemporary note in her writing voice. You'll never realize how hard you're thinking. It'll be too much fun!

DANNAH GRESH, coauthor, *Lies Young Women Believe*, founder, Pure Freedom

in a world gone wild

GIRLS GONE WISE
Companion Guide

MARY A. KASSIAN

MOODY PUBLISHERS
CHICAGO

© 2012 by
MARY A. KASSIAN

Library of Congress Cataloging-in-Publication Data

Kassian, Mary A.
  Girls gone wise companion guide / Mary A. Kassian.
    p. cm.
  ISBN 978-0-8024-5156-9
  I. Christian women--Religious life. I. Kassian, Mary A. Girls gone wise
in a world gone wild. II. Title.
  BV4527.K369 2012
  248.8'43--dc23
                                    2011039650

Edited by Annette LaPlaca
Typesetting: Julia Ryan / www.DesignByJulia.com
Cover design: Faceout Studio
Cover image: RF Shutterstock and Fotolia
Cover photo: JDS Portraits
Author photos: Photography by Katie

                    ISBN: 978-0-8024-5156-9

We hope you enjoy this book from Moody Publishers. Our goal is to provide high quality, thought-provoking books and products that connect truth to your real needs and challenges. For more information on other books and products written and produced from a biblical perspective, go to www.moodypublishers.com or write to:

Moody Publishers
820 N. LaSalle Boulevard
Chicago, IL 60610

5 7 9 10 8 6 4

Printed in the United States of America

CONTENTS

A Message from Mary

I'm so glad that you've decided to study my book *Girls Gone Wise*.

Let me tell you a little bit about me. I turned fifty not too long ago. (My birthday is November II. Send a card. ☺) I'm still planning to go skydiving (although my husband can't understand why). I'm not a granny yet (although I hope it won't be too long). I haven't succumbed to wearing granny shoes (although I must admit that after nursing sore feet, I have been tempted). I've only got a couple of white hairs (I'm hoping that I've inherited my Oma's genes for beautiful snowy-white old-person hair).

I've lived through the feminist movement. (Been there. Done that.) I've gone to University. Got a degree. Had a professional career. Been in a rock band. Studied theology. Written books. I've been married (almost thirty years). Had kids (three boys, one married so far). Loved and followed Jesus since I was young. I've ministered to women for several decades and have spent a lot of time studying the Bible and wrestling with the question of what womanhood is all about.

All that to say: I think I've figured a few things out (not always the easy way!). And I think it's high time that women like me (who have a significant number of miles on our odometers) start teaching women like you (who are just starting out on your journey) what womanhood means and how to make life and relationships work. It's time for us to be spiritual moms.

Unfortunately, the women of the last generation mostly "dropped the ball." We were so busy experimenting with the new ideas about womanhood that feminism fed us that we lost sight of God's amazing design. We lost sight of the most wonderful and precious things about who He created women to be.

The ideas that seemed so wonderful when we were young didn't deliver what they promised. The tragic result of the feminist experiment is that it distracted us women from doing what we ought to have been doing. My generation's experimentation resulted in your generation being "unmothered." Our neglect has produced a swath of spiritually unguided orphans—an era filled with girls gone wild.

Oh, we tried. We gave it our best shot. We thought we had the "smarts" to get it right. We thought we could fix things by deciding for ourselves what womanhood meant and how women (and men) should relate. We were confident we knew best. But history demonstrates that we were wrong. Thinking that we could figure life out for ourselves, without God's direction, was just a sad repetition of the pattern that started in the Garden of Eden with Eve, the first Girl-Gone-Wild.

It's time for a change. It's time for a generation of women who dare to take God at His Word and delight in His plan for male and female. Studying the Bible to learn His plan is what this book is all about. We're not going to try to come up with a new definition of womanhood, like feminism did. Instead, we're going to turn to God, our Creator. We're going to find out what He has to say about womanhood and the way we ought to live. I've discovered that when women turn to the Lord, trust Him, and say yes to His design, broken hearts are mended, fractured lives are healed, and crooked paths are made straight.

Are you ready for the adventure? I hope so. I have been praying for you and will continue to pray for you. You and the young women of your generation are so precious to me. I am asking the Lord to stir your hearts so that the tide will turn. I am praying that by the power of His Spirit, God will start a movement of women who are committed to becoming who He wants them to be. I pray this book will challenge you to the core, change you, and compel you to become part of the quiet counterrevolution of Girls Gone Wise in a world gone wild.

Mary

Mary Kassian

About This Companion Guide

This guide is designed to be a companion study to the book **Girls Gone Wise in a World Gone Wild**. It contains lessons corresponding to each chapter, with questions for personal reflection and application. You will need to have a copy of the book in order to follow along in the study. You do not need to read the entire book before beginning this study; instead, you will be assigned a few pages in the book to read along with each lesson. In this way, you will read the entire book, but in small portions at a time.

The questions in this Companion Guide will help you think about and apply what you are reading. If you do them chapter-by-chapter, completing them right after you've finished reading the corresponding part of the book, the ideas will be fresh in your mind.

Completing each lesson should only take about 10 to 15 minutes. I've included a page after each lesson so you can journal your thoughts and personalize what you've read. I've posted a short book blog video online to accompany each chapter. You can watch them for free by following the links at girlsgonewise.com/ggw. I also invite you to join the thousands of women on the facebook.com/girlsgonewise page.

It's not just over-the-edge, single, college-age girls who qualify as Wild Things. According to Scripture, there is a measure of Girl-Gone-Wildness in all of us.

GGW

Study It with a Friend

One of the best and most fun ways to grow in wisdom is to study the book with someone else. You might study with a friend or a group of friends, create a mom-and-daughter study, or study in a small-group or discipleship setting. That way you can discuss ideas, interact with each other, and encourage each other to apply what you've learned. So why don't you start a Girls-Gone-Wise group?

There's a free leader's guide and several small-group resources available for download on the girlsgonewise.com website. The leader's guide contains suggestions for how to divide the book into a 6-week, 8-week, 12-week, or 22-week study, how to split the study into several modules, or how to just Mix 'n' Match the Points of Contrast that interest you. You can download and customize the plan that works best for your group. We've tried to make the options as flexible as possible, so you can pick and choose and adapt the material to meet your needs. You can also purchase an optional leader's kit to enrich your small-group study. The leader's kit contains a DVD with dozens of short, discussion-provoking video clips: There are person-on-the-street interviews, testimonies from various women, table-talk with Kay Arthur, video segments where viewers will "Get It from the Guys," and segments where I introduce the study and wrap things up. The video clips enhance the study by providing "teasers" to stimulate discussion. The DVD also contains printable graphics and a promo video to help you promote your group. If you're interested, we've also got some funky Girls Gone Wise latte mugs, pins, and bags available. You can find out more about all the available resources by visiting GirlsGoneWise.com/ggw.

Every woman is called to be a spiritual "mom." You are never too young. It's never too early to start influencing your girlfriends to walk on the path of life. So grab a friend. Meet at your kitchen table, at Starbucks, at school, on campus, or wherever. Studying what God has to say about womanhood will help you and your girlfriends build successful relationships God's way and avoid the heartache that comes from going wild.

Getting Started

Take your time as you do these lessons. The questions are meant to challenge you and force you to think through your attitudes and beliefs about womanhood and relationships. Some of the questions may be painful. To be honest, I hope they are. Without pain, you won't be motivated to change; and without change, you cannot hope to grow in wisdom. As you sense God working in your heart, I suggest that you pause and spend time in prayer, to allow the Holy Spirit to speak to you and teach you what He wants you to learn. Remember, the more you put into the study, the more you'll get out of it. As you faithfully read and work through the lessons and seek to apply them to your life, I believe the Lord will faithfully transform you—and change you from a Girl-Gone-Wild into a breathtakingly beautiful Girl-Gone-Wise.

Are you ready to get started? Read the introduction, entitled "Wild Thing," in **Girls Gone Wise**, on pages 9–20. Then come back to this Companion Guide and answer the questions that relate to the introduction.

 Don't forget to check out Mary's blog, and all the other resources that are available on the website at www.girlsgonewise.com

Wild Thing

She Could Be *You*

"Look carefully then how you walk,
not as unwise [wild] but as wise."
(Ephesians 5:15)

Read the introduction of **Girls Gone Wise** (pages 9–20).

THE MAIN POINT

There's really nothing new about girls going wild.
The Bible paints a portrait of the prototypical wild woman.
It also paints a portrait of the prototypical wise woman.
Both types of girls—Wild Things and Wise Things—have
existed throughout history. A Girl-Gone-Wild is a woman
who relies on her own know-how rather than relying on God.
She neglects or disregards what God has to say about the
way she ought to live and chooses instead to do her
own thing, her own way. This was the mistake of Eve—
the first Girl-Gone-Wild—who went with her own
gut instinct instead of trusting and obeying the Lord.
Scripture teaches that there's a measure of wildness in
all of us. Because of sin, "wild" is our default setting.
The pull to be wild is incredibly strong. To be wise,
you need to put in the necessary time and effort to
counteract this pull. You need to intentionally seek
and welcome God's input.

1. Jot down a list of possible reasons the young married woman of Proverbs 7 went "wild."

_____

_____

2. Do you think you have little or much in common with the Wild Thing of Proverbs 7? Explain why.

_____

_____

_____

God's grace is bigger than all of our sin. The power of Christ can transform even the most messed-up and broken Wild Thing into a Girl-Gone-Wise.

GGW

3. The book equates "wild" with what Scripture calls foolish, wayward, evil, ignorant, or unwise. Look up the definition of "wild" in a dictionary. Write down the dictionary definition that best captures the nature of a Girl-Gone-Wild.

_____

_____

4. In your own words, what's the definition of a Girl-Gone-Wise?

_____

_____

5. Describe a situation when, like Eve and the Proverbs 7 Wild Thing, Satan tempted you to view the "forbidden fruit" of sin as attractive, harmless, and incredibly promising.

_____

_____

6. What negative consequences did or could have resulted from indulging in that forbidden fruit?

_____

_____

7. Proverbs 1:22 talks about 3 types of wild people. Do you see any of these three types of "wildness" in your own heart? (Check all that apply)

☐ Apathy: Being unwilling to learn or do what is right (Simple)

☐ Resistance: Shrugging off God's input and standards (Fool)

☐ Rebellion: Being insolent and willfully disobedient (Scoffer)

8. In your Bible, read Proverbs 8:11. Summarize what this verse teaches about the value of wisdom.

_____

_____

9. On the journaling page, write out a prayer, asking the Lord to help you do what it takes to treasure wisdom and to pursue becoming a Girl-Gone-Wise.

I've created short videos to accompany each chapter. You can view them on the **Girls Gone Wise** website at girlsgonewise.com/ggw. Just follow the link to the video book blog. Make sure to check out the website and Facebook page. You'll find my blog and lots of other great resources to help you get spiritual smarts for life and love.

Use this page to journal. Write down what you're learning. Record your thoughts, comments, favorite verse, quotes, or questions. Compose a prayer, letter, or poem. Jot down notes from your small-group session. Draw, doodle, or diagram. Be creative. We've provided this space so you can process and apply the book whichever way is best for you.

Remember: You'll find videos, a forum, and many other resources to help you learn how to walk wisely on the GirlsGoneWise.com website. And you can follow Girls Gone Wise on Facebook (facebook.com/girlsgone-wise) and Twitter (twitter.com/girlsgonewise) too.

HEART

What Holds First Place in Your Affections?

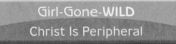

Girl-Gone-**WILD**	Girl-Gone-**WISE**
Christ Is Peripheral	Christ Is Central

"Her feet go down to death; her steps follow the path to Sheol; she does not ponder the path of life; her ways wander, and she does not know it."

(Proverbs 5:5–6)

"Her heart has not turned back, nor have her steps departed from your way."

(Psalm 44:18)

Read pages 23–33 in the *Girls Gone Wise* book.

THE MAIN POINT

The writer of Proverbs says you can tell a lot about a girl by the way she walks. He advised his son to check out a woman's feet— that is, her behavior; the way she acts and talks, conducts herself, and the choices she makes—in order to get an idea of the inner state of her *heart*. A girl's feet and her heart are closely connected. If her *heart* is in love with the Lord Jesus, her *feet* will demonstrate her devotion. A *Wise Thing* gives the Lord Jesus Christ first place in her heart. Her feet follow the inclination of her heart, so she makes cautious, wise, godly decisions about her relationships with men. A *Wild Thing*, on the other hand, does not have Christ at the center of her affections. Because of this, she makes missteps in her relationship with men. "Her ways wander, and she doesn't know it." What do your feet say about you? If the Sage Father were to watch you walk, would He peg you as a Girl-Gone-Wild or a Girl-Gone-Wise?

1. Reread Proverbs 5:5–6 and Psalm 44:18 on the previous page. According to these verses, how does the "way" of a Wild Thing differ from that of a Wise Thing?

_____

_____

_____

2. In your own words, explain what the Bible means when it refers to a woman's "walk."

_____

_____

_____

Girls **GONE** *Wise*

A girl's walk has to do with the overriding inclination of her heart. Her walk demonstrates where her loyalty lies. It reveals whether her heart is inclined toward the Lord or toward other things.

GGW

3. What does a woman's "walk" reveal about her?

☐ What type of shoes she's wearing

☐ Which direction she's headed

☐ The inclination of her heart

☐ Where her loyalty lies

☐ Whether she is wild or wise

4. Look up and read the following verses in your Bible. Draw lines to match each reference to the thought it contains:

Deuteronomy 11:21–23   If we love Jesus, we will do what He says.

John 14:15   Blessing and victory come from loving God, walking in all His ways, and holding fast to Him.

2 John 1:5–6   From the beginning, the Lord has stressed the importance of the heart-foot connection; love means walking in obedience.

5. If the Sage Father were to evaluate your "steps"—the way you think, talk, act, and all the small, daily choices you make—would He peg you as more wild or more wise? Why?

_____

_____

6. Take an honest look inside. Put a mark on the scale below to indicate how close you hold Christ to your heart's center:

| | | | | | | | | | | | | | | | | | | | | | | | | | | | | | | | | | | | |

Christ is not at the center of my heart.   Christ is at the center of my heart.
My ways wander.   I try to follow all His ways.

7. What things most compete for that center spot in your affections?

_____

_____

8. What adjustments do you need to make to allow room for Christ to take His rightful place in your heart?

_____

_____

9. The Lord will help you change, if you truly want to. Write out a personalized version of God's promise by inserting your name in each blank.

"I will give _____ a new heart, and a new spirit I will put

within _____. And I will remove the heart of stone from

_____'s flesh and give _____ a heart of flesh.

And I will put my Spirit within _____, and cause

_____ to walk in my statutes and be careful to obey my rules."

(Ezekiel 36:26–28)

**Using this verse, ask the Lord to give you a new heart
and to help you walk in His way.**

Use this page to journal. Write down what you're learning. Record your thoughts, comments, favorite verse, quotes, or questions. Compose a prayer, letter, or poem. Jot down notes from your small-group session. Draw, doodle, or diagram. Be creative. We've provided this space so you can process and apply the book whichever way is best for you.

Remember: You'll find videos, a forum, and many other resources to help you learn how to walk wisely on the GirlsGoneWise.com website. And you can follow Girls Gone Wise on Facebook (facebook.com/girlsgone-wise) and Twitter (twitter.com/girlsgonewise) too.

COUNSEL

Where Do You Get Your Instruction?

Girl-Gone-**WILD**	Girl-Gone-**WISE**
World-Instructed	Word-Instructed

"Her feet go down to death; her steps follow the path to Sheol; she does not ponder the path of life; her ways wander, and she does not know it."

(Proverbs 5:5–6)

"She walks not in the counsel of the wicked, nor stands in the way of sinners, nor sits in the seat of scoffers; but her delight is in the law of the Lord, and on his law she meditates day and night."

(Psalm 1:1–2)

Read pages 35–44 in the *Girls Gone Wise* book.

THE MAIN POINT

A Wild Thing doesn't ponder the path of life. She goes about her daily business and neglects to consider the way of the Lord. It's not that she willfully snubs God's way. She just doesn't take the time or make the effort to figure out what it is or how to walk in it. Instead, the ideas of the world get into her system and numb her sensibilities. Her constant exposure to mass media poisons the way she thinks and behaves. The problem with popular media is that it constantly lies about the nature of truth, goodness, and beauty. It offers counterfeit versions of what womanhood, male-female relationships, romance, sexuality, marriage, and family are all about. It typically portrays sin as natural and harmless. And if you're frequently exposed to that message, that's what you're going to believe. Wise Things are careful about where they get their relationship advice. If you want to be wise, you'll intentionally tune out the false messages of the world, and make an effort to tune in to the truth of the Word instead.

1. Write down the names of the last 3 TV shows and/or movies you watched and the last 3 magazines you read.

_____

_____

_____

2. Did any of these shows, movies and/or magazines:

Characterize sex outside of marriage as normal or desirable?	☐ YES	☐ NO
Characterize homosexuality as normal or desirable?	☐ YES	☐ NO
Cast marriage in a negative light?	☐ YES	☐ NO
Cast men in a negative light?	☐ YES	☐ NO
Cast children in a negative light?	☐ YES	☐ NO
Portray women as defiant or sexually aggressive?	☐ YES	☐ NO
Suggest that worth is based on physical beauty?	☐ YES	☐ NO
Imply that a woman's worth is based on her career?	☐ YES	☐ NO
Encourage immodesty or greed?	☐ YES	☐ NO
Mock morality or Christian faith?	☐ YES	☐ NO
Minimize the consequences of sin?	☐ YES	☐ NO

3. Do you agree with the statement "You will become what you expose yourself to"? Explain why or why not.

_____

_____

_____

4. Fill in the flow chart describing how compromise usually happens (see the example about Eve in _GGW_, page 40).

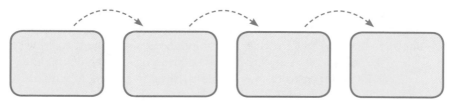

5. Has your tolerance level for viewing sinful images increased or decreased over the past 5 years? Explain:

_____

_____

6. Can you identify other ways popular media have affected your thinking?

_____

_____

_____

7. According to Philippians 4:8, what types of things ought you to be filling your mind with?

_____

_____

_____

Girls **Wise**
GONE

A woman who neglects God's way will begin to walk the world's way. It's bound to happen. She'll become what she is exposed to.
GGW

8. Do your media choices demonstrate that you are carefully pondering the path of life? What adjustments do you need to make?

_____

_____

Take the Girls Gone Wise Media Challenge . . .

For the next week, keep a log of all the "counsel" you expose yourself to. Then figure out the percentage of godly versus benign/ungodly counsel. [Benign and ungodly seem to make a strange pair. Check the book!]

 If you want to do something really radical, surf on over to girlsgone-wise.com and sign up for the 30-day media reduction challenge.

Use this page to journal. Write down what you're learning. Record your thoughts, comments, favorite verse, quotes, or questions. Compose a prayer, letter, or poem. Jot down notes from your small-group session. Draw, doodle, or diagram. Be creative. We've provided this space so you can process and apply the book whichever way is best for you.

Remember: You'll find videos, a forum, and many other resources to help you learn how to walk wisely on the GirlsGoneWise.com website. And you can follow Girls Gone Wise on Facebook (facebook.com/girlsgone-wise) and Twitter (twitter.com/girlsgonewise) too.

APPROACH

Who Directs Your Love Story?

Girl-Gone-**WILD**	Girl-Gone-**WISE**
Self-Manipulated	God-Orchestrated

"And behold, the woman meets him . . . *wily of heart.*"
(Proverbs 7:10)

She trusts in the Lord with all her heart, and does not lean on her own understanding. In all her ways she acknowledges Him and He makes her paths straight.
(Proverbs 3:5–6, NIV)

Read pages 45–55 in the **Girls Gone Wise** book.

THE MAIN POINT

Relying on her "wiles" is the approach a Girl-Gone-Wild takes in relationships. She's calculating—exceptionally clever in the craft of manipulation. She uses all sorts of tricks and schemes to insidiously entice and entrap. She knows how to flirt, seduce, admire, compliment, pout, cry, reason, argue, lie, accuse, nag, plot, and do whatever else is necessary to achieve her goal. Desire and obsession have gripped her. She's a living, breathing example of Want. The Wild Thing tries to sit in the director's chair and manipulate the scene so her man will do what she wants. She tries to direct his behavior and control the outcome of their story. The Girl-Gone-Wise takes a different approach—a radically different approach. She does not play the manipulation game. She takes her hands off the director's chair, relinquishes control, and trusts God to orchestrate her life's script.

I. In the word cloud, circle three words that are not associated with what it means to be "wily."

CUNNING **Unpretentious** **Designing**
HONEST *Sneaky* *Calculating* Scheming CRAFTY
DEVIOUS **Forthright** *Sly* Tricky

2. What are some specific ways our culture encourages women to manipulate men?

_____

_____

3. Rank the following types of manipulation from I to 5, with I being the type of manipulation you've used the most, to 5 being the type of manipulation you've used the least:

_____ Sexual Manipulation

_____ Verbal Manipulation

_____ Emotional Manipulation

_____ Spiritual Manipulation

_____ Circumstantial Manipulation

4. Can you describe an instance when being wily has blown up in your face?

_____

_____

5. Why does wily behavior demonstrate a disdain for truth?

_____

_____

6. What else does a wily approach to relationships demonstrate? (check all that apply)

☐ That we don't trust the Lord

☐ That we think we know best

☐ That we've watched too many Looney Tunes cartoons.

☐ That we are control freaks

☐ That we are trying to play God

7. Why is it difficult for women to refrain from taking a wily approach to relationships?

_____

_____

8. Reread Proverbs 3:5–6. How well are you putting this verse into practice when it comes to your approach to relationships? Explain.

_____

_____

_____

Girls GONE *Wise*

The Lord wants you to taste and see that HE is good—and that good things happen when you stop being wily and trust Him with your love story.
GGW

9. How can you become less wily and increasingly wise?

_____

_____

_____

Use this page to journal. Write down what you're learning. Record your thoughts, comments, favorite verse, quotes, or questions. Compose a prayer, letter, or poem. Jot down notes from your small-group session. Draw, doodle, or diagram. Be creative. We've provided this space so you can process and apply the book whichever way is best for you.

Remember: You'll find videos, a forum, and many other resources to help you learn how to walk wisely on the GirlsGoneWise.com website. And you can follow Girls Gone Wise on Facebook (facebook.com/girlsgone-wise) and Twitter (twitter.com/girlsgonewise) too.

ATTITUDE

Your Prevailing Disposition

Girl-Gone-**WILD**	Girl-Gone-**WISE**
Clamorous & Defiant	Gentle, Calm, Amenable

"She is loud and wayward . . ." (Proverbs 7:11)	Her heart reflects the imperishable beauty of a gentle and quiet spirit, which in God's sight is very precious. (I Peter 3:4)

Read pages 57–69 in the **Girls Gone Wise** book.

THE MAIN POINT

The Sage pegs the Wild Thing as "loud" and "wayward." In other words, she's a sassy, defiant, my-way-or-the-highway kind of a girl. If she were alive today, she'd fit right in. In fact, she'd probably make it to the cover of *Cosmopolitan*, or be a candidate for a woman of the year award, or be featured in the Who's Who of Forbes's Most Powerful Women, or maybe be hired by Hollywood to be the next sexy, aggressive, karate-chopping, gun-slinging, male-kicking female star. The clamorous, defiant attitude of the Girl-Gone-Wild stands in marked contrast to the soft, receptive disposition the Lord intended for women. Scripture teaches that the Girl-Gone-Wise is characterized by a gentle, calm, amenable womanly disposition, which is incredibly beautiful and very precious to God.

The beautiful softness of womanhood was severely damaged when Eve sinned, but the Bible directs us to reclaim the beauty of our original created design.

I. Imagine the following two models of womanhood:

EXHIBIT A: She's a tough, sassy, sexy, independent career woman.

EXHIBIT B: She's a calm, sweet, submissive, nurturing housewife and mom.

On a purely emotional level, which model of womanhood seems more appealing to you?

Which seems more glamorous?	☐ **A**	☐ **B**
Which seems more interesting?	☐ **A**	☐ **B**
Which seems more exciting?	☐ **A**	☐ **B**
Which seems more desirable?	☐ **A**	☐ **B**

2. Overall, which model of womanhood do you find more compelling, and why?

_____

_____

3. Proverbs describes the Wild Thing as "loud" and "wayward." Refer to pages 60–61 in *Girls Gone Wise* to complete the following chart:

A "loud" woman is . . .	A "wayward" woman is . . .

4. How often do you exhibit a clamorous ("You'd better do it my way!") or defiant ("I refuse to do it your way!") attitude?

☐ Never   ☐ Rarely   ☐ Occasionally   ☐ Often   ☐ Habitually

5. How do you feel about the fact that Adam associated manhood with "strength" and womanhood with "softness"?

_____

_____

6. Read I Peter 3:3-6. How does God's assessment of the womanly traits of gentleness, calmness, and amenability compare with the world's assessment of the ideal disposition for women?

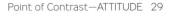

According to Scripture, it's woman's softness, her ability to receive, respond, and relate, that is her greatest strength.

GGW

_____

_____

_____

7. What factors might keep you from becoming increasingly gentle, calm, and amenable?

_____

_____

_____

8. How committed are you to pursuing the disposition of a Girl-Gone-Wise?

_____

_____

Use this page to journal. Write down what you're learning. Record your thoughts, comments, favorite verse, quotes, or questions. Compose a prayer, letter, or poem. Jot down notes from your small-group session. Draw, doodle, or diagram. Be creative. We've provided this space so you can process and apply the book whichever way is best for you.

Remember: You'll find videos, a forum, and many other resources to help you learn how to walk wisely on the GirlsGoneWise.com website. And you can follow Girls Gone Wise on Facebook (facebook.com/girlsgone-wise) and Twitter (twitter.com/girlsgonewise) too.

HABITS

Your Priorities and Routines

Girl-Gone-**WILD**	Girl-Gone-**WISE**
Self-Indulgent	Self-Disciplined

"Her feet do not stay
at home; now in the street,
now in the market,
and at every corner."

(Proverbs 7:11–12)

"She looks well to the
ways of her household
and does not eat the
bread of idleness."

(Proverbs 31:27)

Read pages 71–82 in the *Girls Gone Wise* book.

THE MAIN POINT

The habits of a Wise Thing are very different from the habits of
the Wild Thing. Both are busy. But they are busy with different
things. The Wild Thing is busy indulging herself. She is constantly
out-and-about, looking for a good time, and she neglects things on
the home front. The Girl-Gone-Wise attends to her home life.
She puts first things first. Her habits are self-disciplined,
self-sacrificing, and directed by the needs of her household.
"Her feet stay at home." Our home is our private sanctum.
It's the "place"—physically and spiritually—where the most
important stuff in life happens. Home is crucial. If a woman's
surroundings are neglected, out-of-order, cluttered, and chaotic,
chances are her inner, private life shares the same fate.
The Bible teaches that God created woman with a uniquely
feminine "bent" for the home. Creating a home is on its
Top Ten list of important things that older women
need to teach the younger ones how to do.

I. How does constantly being "out-and-about" contribute to a woman being a Girl-Gone-Wild?

_____

_____

2. Make a list of the habits and disciplines that you think a wise woman aims to incorporate into her life.

_____

_____

_____

_____

_____

Homeward-faced,
Wisdom-graced.
Out-to-the-max,
Wisdom lacks.
GGW

3. Based on your habits, what are your top 5 priorities?

_____

_____

_____

_____

_____

4. What things distract you from having a heart for your home?

_____

_____

_____

_____

5. Compare your habits to the habits of a Wise Thing. Evaluate to what extent each statement describes you:

Her habits are self-disciplined and not self-indulgent.

1	2	3	4	5	6	7	8	9	10

This does NOT describe me.   This accurately describes me.

She habitually attends to matters of personal faith and character.

1	2	3	4	5	6	7	8	9	10

This does NOT describe me.   This accurately describes me.

She habitually attends to the needs of her household.

1	2	3	4	5	6	7	8	9	10

This does NOT describe me.   This accurately describes me.

She habitually attends to Kingdom mission and ministry.

1	2	3	4	5	6	7	8	9	10

This does NOT describe me.   This accurately describes me.

She habitually attends to beneficial (and not idle) pursuits.

1	2	3	4	5	6	7	8	9	10

This does NOT describe me.   This accurately describes me.

She and her household reap the reward of her disciplined lifestyle.

1	2	3	4	5	6	7	8	9	10

This does NOT describe me.   This accurately describes me.

6. What adjustments do you need to make to ensure that your priorities are in the right order?

_____

_____

Use this page to journal. Write down what you're learning. Record your thoughts, comments, favorite verse, quotes, or questions. Compose a prayer, letter, or poem. Jot down notes from your small-group session. Draw, doodle, or diagram. Be creative. We've provided this space so you can process and apply the book whichever way is best for you.

Remember: You'll find videos, a forum, and many other resources to help you learn how to walk wisely on the GirlsGoneWise.com website. And you can follow Girls Gone Wise on Facebook (facebook.com/girlsgonewise) and Twitter (twitter.com/girlsgonewise) too.

FOCUS

What Commands Your Attention?

Girl-Gone-**WILD**	Girl-Gone-**WISE**
Getting	Giving

"She lies in wait."
(Proverbs 7:12)

"She opens her hand
to the poor and
reaches out her
hands to the needy."
(Proverbs 31:20)

Read pages 83–92 in the *Girls Gone Wise* book.

THE MAIN POINT

The Bible uses a hunting metaphor to describe the behavior of the Wild Thing. It says she "lies in wait." In this instance, her prey was a man. But lying-in-wait behavior isn't restricted to getting a guy. It extends to getting other things, too. The Wild Thing may lie in wait to get the house, get the car, get new clothes, get a job, get kids, get a break, get her way, or get her husband to change. Get this. Get that. Many women spend their whole lives lying in wait. They perpetually wait and watch for their next big catch and hope it will bring them the fulfillment they so desperately desire. Their predatory behavior stands in marked contrast to the productive behavior of a Girl-Gone-Wise. A Wise Thing doesn't waste time "lying in wait." Time is too precious. There's far too much to be done and accomplished for Jesus. She's on a mission. She has a *Kingdom focus* instead of a *me focus*. She's far more concerned about what she can give than what she can get.

1. In the space below, make a list of things women commonly want/desire:

_____

_____

2. Can you identify something(s) you are currently "lying in wait" for?

_____

_____

3. At what point does the pursuit of a legitimate desire change from being wise to wild? Check all that apply:

☐ When getting what we want becomes an obsession

☐ When the pursuit of what we want consumes all our time and energy

☐ When we stake our identity or happiness on getting what we want

☐ When we neglect other things we ought to be doing

☐ When we try to meet a legitimate need in an illegitimate way

☐ When chasing what we want distracts us from our mission and calling

☐ When our own needs are all we can see or think about

☐ Other: _____

4. Describe a time when you went "wild" in pursuing a desire. Which of the behaviors listed in question 3 did you exhibit?

_____

_____

5. Proverbs 1:18 indicates that lying in wait sucks the life out of a predator, and that she will ultimately hurt herself. How have you (or how might you) hurt yourself by lying in wait?

_____

_____

6. What "one thing" did the following people focus on (or fail to focus on)?

David (Psalm 27:4) _____

Mary (Luke 10:42) _____

Paul (Philippians 3:13–14) _____

Rich Young Man (Mark 10:21) _____

7. To what extent is your desire to get what you identified in question #2 distracting you from focusing on what the Lord would want you to focus on?

_____

_____

8. What Kingdom business can you do this week? Jot down something that you think the Lord wants you to do for someone. Or ask the Lord for an opportunity to "give," then keep your eyes open and seize the opportunity when it comes.

_____

_____

_____

Girls **Wise**
GONE

She focuses on building Christ's Kingdom—not on building her own— and that makes a major difference in how she interacts with men.

GGW

9. On the journaling page, describe how you "gave" and note how it made you feel. Did looking out for the needs of others change your focus? Did it pull your attention away from lying in wait?

Use this page to journal. Write down what you're learning. Record your thoughts, comments, favorite verse, quotes, or questions. Compose a prayer, letter, or poem. Jot down notes from your small-group session. Draw, doodle, or diagram. Be creative. We've provided this space so you can process and apply the book whichever way is best for you.

Remember: You'll find videos, a forum, and many other resources to help you learn how to walk wisely on the GirlsGoneWise.com website. And you can follow Girls Gone Wise on Facebook (facebook.com/girlsgone-wise) and Twitter (twitter.com/girlsgonewise) too.

APPEARANCE

How You Adorn Yourself

Girl-Gone-**WILD**	Girl-Gone-**WISE**
Unbecoming, Indecent, Excessive	Becoming, Decent, Moderate

"And behold, the woman meets him, dressed as a prostitute." (Proverbs 7:10)	She adorns herself "in respectable apparel, with modesty and self-control." (I Timothy 2:9)

Read pages 93–107 in the **Girls Gone Wise** book.

THE MAIN POINT

Among Christians, discussions about women's clothing are often reduced to the question of the best way to help men avoid temptation. But curbing wrongful sexual activity is not the main reason behind the Bible's teaching on modesty. There's far more to it than that. Clothing is an outward, visible symbol of an inward, spiritual reality. We wear clothes because we have lost the glory and beauty of our original sin-free selves. Clothes are a symbol that testify to the fact that we need to "wear Christ" in order to be presentable to God. That's why we wear them. And that's why dressing in a way that exposes and draws attention to our nakedness is shameful. In the final analysis, your clothing is not meant to be about you—it's meant to display deep and profound spiritual truths about the gospel. That's why it's highly important that you wrestle with the practical question of what to wear and what not to wear.

I. Explain what it means to dress "as a prostitute" (see *GGW*, pages 94–95).

_____

_____

2. Have you ever been guilty of dressing "as a prostitute"? If you had a different body type, would you be tempted to? Why or why not?

_____

_____

3. When you were young, did your parents have any rules for the way you dressed? Can you think of a time when you disagreed with them over your appearance?

Spiritual adornment is the reality. Physical adornment is the symbol of that reality. The external clothing we wear is of secondary importance. But it is important nonetheless.

GGW

_____

_____

_____

_____

4. Briefly explain what you were taught about why girls should or should not cover up their bodies.

_____

_____

5. In your own words, summarize what the Bible teaches about why we wear clothes.

_____

_____

6. Choose and copy a quote from the chapter that best reflects the idea of why adequately covering up our nakedness is necessary.

_____

_____

_____

7. Does the concept that your clothing is meant to display deep and profound spiritual truths about the gospel change the way you think about the way you dress? How?

_____

_____

8. The second paragraph on _GGW_ page 102 mentions some common pitfalls surrounding the practical question of what to and what not to wear. Which of these pitfalls have tripped you up?

_____

_____

9. How do you think applying the three standards ("Is it becoming?" "Is it decent?" "Is it moderate?") would affect your choice of clothing, accessories, and makeup?

_____

_____

Use this page to journal. Write down what you're learning. Record your thoughts, comments, favorite verse, quotes, or questions. Compose a prayer, letter, or poem. Jot down notes from your small-group session. Draw, doodle, or diagram. Be creative. We've provided this space so you can process and apply the book whichever way is best for you.

Remember: You'll find videos, a forum, and many other resources to help you learn how to walk wisely on the GirlsGoneWise.com website. And you can follow Girls Gone Wise on Facebook (facebook.com/girlsgone-wise) and Twitter (twitter.com/girlsgonewise) too.

BODY LANGUAGE
Your Nonverbal Behavior

Girl-Gone-**WILD**	Girl-Gone-**WISE**
Suggestive	Demure

She captures him with her eyelashes.
(Proverbs 6:25)

". . . graceful and of deadly charms."
(Nahum 3:4)

She does not resort to deceitful charm.
(Proverbs 31:30)

Read pages 109–118 in the **Girls Gone Wise** book.

THE MAIN POINT

Women's magazines commonly teach women how to flirt.
They provide suggestions, or even step-by-step instructions,
on how to use nonverbal body language to charm and turn men on.
But according to God's Word, not even a hint of sexual immorality
or impurity is appropriate among believers. *Not even a hint!* That
means that even the tiniest allusion, suggestion, or whiff of sexual
"naughtiness" is *not* okay. The sultry look and provocative pose may
impress the guys, but it doesn't impress the Lord. A Girl-Gone-Wise
takes God's disdain for sensuality seriously. She does not engage
in inappropriate, sexually charged flirtatious communication.
She doesn't hint—even by way of playful innuendo—that evil is
desirable. She is very, very careful to avoid any look or behavior
that sends this ungodly message. She keeps her body language in
check: modest, reserved, and free of impure sexual undertones.

1. What's the difference between a woman who is truly charming and a woman who deceptively tries to charm? (See *GGW*, page 113.)

_____

_____

2. What do women who flirt hope to accomplish by it?

_____

_____

3. Put a check mark beside all the messages that flirty provocative body language conveys.

☐ "I find you sexually attractive."

☐ "Does my body entice you?"

☐ "I want to arouse your sexual interest."

☐ "Do you want to get it on with me?"

☐ "I'm not thinking about sex right now."

☐ "Imagine what I look like naked."

☐ "Come and get me."

☐ "It would be fun to mess around."

☐ "Let's take this further."

☐ "I'm available" or "I might be available."

☐ "Being sexually naughty is fun."

Girls GONE *Wise*

Seduction is any behavior that purposefully leads another person in the wrong direction. It's any behavior that falsely hints that evil is desirable or exciting.

GGW

4. What would you say to the argument that flirting is just teasing— that it's just for fun and not really serious?

_____

_____

5. Read Ephesians 5:3–4. Explain why suggestive body language displeases the Lord.

_____

_____

6. Explain why a wife's suggestive body language toward her husband does not fall into this category.

_____

_____

7. Do you intentionally send out nonverbal invitations for men to look and lust? Put a mark on the scale to indicate how close your nonverbal behavior comes to Paul's "Zero Tolerance" policy of "not even a hint of sexual immorality or of any kind of impurity" being proper for God's people.

I	2	3	4	5	6	7	8	9	10

My behavior never
hints at impurity.

My behavior often
hints at impurity.

8. How does the Bible's condemnation of sensuality as sin compare to the world's perspective on sensuality?

_____

_____

9. Do you need to repent of the sin of sensuality? Or, if you are married, do you need to increase your sexually inviting body language toward your husband? On your journaling page, write down how you will apply this chapter to your life.

Use this page to journal. Write down what you're learning. Record your thoughts, comments, favorite verse, quotes, or questions. Compose a prayer, letter, or poem. Jot down notes from your small-group session. Draw, doodle, or diagram. Be creative. We've provided this space so you can process and apply the book whichever way is best for you.

Remember: You'll find videos, a forum, and many other resources to help you learn how to walk wisely on the GirlsGoneWise.com website. And you can follow Girls Gone Wise on Facebook (facebook.com/girlsgone-wise) and Twitter (twitter.com/girlsgonewise) too.

ROLES

Your Pattern of Interaction

Girl-Gone-**WILD**	Girl-Gone-**WISE**
Inclined to Dominate	Inclined to Follow

"She seizes him. . . .
He follows her."
(Proverbs 7:13, 22)

Like Sarah, she submits
to her husband and to
God's beautiful design.
(I Peter 3:4–6)

Read pages II9–I34 in the *Girls Gone Wise* book.

THE MAIN POINT

Culture's portrayal of the ideal woman has changed drastically over the past few decades. In the 1950s, the ideal woman was portrayed as a sweet wife and stay-at-home mom who doted on her husband and kids, baked cookies, and enjoyed vacuuming. Nowadays, the ideal woman is portrayed as a sassy, brash, sexually salacious, fiercely independent career woman who refuses to be defined by husband or family. So we've exchanged one stereotype for another. The problem is that "who we are" is not a matter decided by us—but by the One who in the beginning created us male and female. According to the Bible, you can *discover* the purpose of your existence—but you can't *dictate* it. Your Creator defines who you are and what your womanhood is all about. He doesn't give you a checklist for what exactly your life must look like, but He does give you very clear principles about the purpose and meaning of womanhood and how to live your life in a manner that glorifies God.

1. Read Ephesians 5:22–33. According to verses 31–32, after what did the Lord pattern the relationship between the first husband and wife?

_____

_____

2. List some ways the roles of Adam and Eve foreshadowed Christ's relationship to the Church.

_____

_____

_____

Girls Gone Wise

> The truth that God wanted to display through male and female was of paramount importance. So it stands to reason that He was highly intentional when He created them.
> *GGW*

3. Why do you think God chose male and female as His canvas to put the relationship between Christ and the church on display?

_____

_____

_____

4. What does it mean that woman was created "for" man? What does it NOT mean?

_____

_____

5. How do the physical bodies of men and women reflect the fact that God created men with a bent to initiate, provide, and protect and women with a bent to respond, relate, and receive?

_____

_____

6. How has sin affected the God-given bent of each sex?

_____

_____

7. Why do you think our culture reacts negatively to the idea of differing roles and responsibilities for male and female?

_____

_____

8. Proverbs 7 reveals that a Wild Thing "seizes" a man and compels him to "follow her." How common is this pattern in contemporary male-female relationships?

_____

_____

9. Do you need to make any adjustments in the way you interact with men to bring your behavior more in line with God's created design?

_____

_____

10. Does your heart resonate and agree with God that His creation of male and female is "very good"? On your journaling page, write a letter to God, telling Him how you feel about male-female roles.

Use this page to journal. Write down what you're learning. Record your thoughts, comments, favorite verse, quotes, or questions. Compose a prayer, letter, or poem. Jot down notes from your small-group session. Draw, doodle, or diagram. Be creative. We've provided this space so you can process and apply the book whichever way is best for you.

Remember: You'll find videos, a forum, and many other resources to help you learn how to walk wisely on the GirlsGoneWise.com website. And you can follow Girls Gone Wise on Facebook (facebook.com/girlsgone-wise) and Twitter (twitter.com/girlsgonewise) too.

SEXUAL CONDUCT

Your Sexual Behavior

Girl-Gone-**WILD**
Impure & Dishonorable

Girl-Gone-**WISE**
Pure & Honorable

". . . and kisses him."
(Proverbs 7:13)

She controls her body
in holiness and honor
and does not wrong
her brother.
(I Thessalonians 4:4–6)

Read pages 135–150 in the **Girls Gone Wise** book.

THE MAIN POINT

We can't hope to get our sexual conduct right until we understand
what sex is all about. God created manhood, womanhood, marriage,
and sex to put on display Christ's cosmic romance with the church.
Human love relationships are based on the story of the Bridegroom
who loved His bride so much that He died to redeem her, the
story of how wonderful their wedding and eternal union will be.
Our sexuality and sexual conduct are ultimately not about us.
They exist to bear witness to Christ's covenant relationship with
the Church. Understanding that marriage and sex exist to display
the covenant commitment, love, unity, permanency, and exclusivity
of Christ's relationship to the Church answers a whole lot of
questions about what is and what isn't appropriate sexual behavior.
Your conduct here on earth is to physically mirror the purity of
that eternal, spiritual relationship. Sex is one of the ways
you can faithfully tell the story of Christ.

1. How would the average person on the street answer the question, "Why did God create sex?" Ask a few friends, neighbors, or coworkers. Jot down a list of possible answers.

_____

_____

2. Why did God create sex? Refer to pages 142–143 in *Girls Gone Wise*. In the space below, copy the quote (or quotes) that best explain why God created sex, or summarize the reason in your own words.

_____

_____

3. Given the biblical meaning of sex, why is it wrong for a man and woman who are not married to one another to be physically intimate?

_____

_____

4. How does an unmarried woman honor the true meaning of sex with her sexual behavior?

_____

_____

_____

Girls GONE *Wise*

God wants us to understand the cosmic, amazing meaning of sex and to honor that meaning with all our hearts.

GGW

5. How does a married woman honor the true meaning of sex with her sexual behavior?

_____

_____

_____

6. Paul's crash course in Sexual Conduct 101 is found in 1 Thessalonians 4:1–8. Read the passage in your Bible or on page 146 of *Girls Gone Wise*. Then, give yourself a "grade" (**A** to **F**) for how well your sexual conduct meets the Bible's standard.

Grade A-F	Sexual Conduct Report Card
	I have abstained from sexual immorality in every thought, word, and deed.
	I continually aim for a higher standard of purity and to improve the way my sexuality tells the gospel story.
	I have controlled my body in holiness and honor.
	I have not sexually defrauded men. I have not inappropriately flirted with them, worn suggestive clothing, tempted them, or wronged them.
	I have not neglected the importance of my sexual conduct. My sexuality accurately reflects the gospel story.

Don't despair if you didn't get a very good grade. The jaw-dropping message of the gospel is that Jesus died to pay for all our mistakes. He doesn't condemn us. He suffered and died so that we might experience His abundant grace and forgiveness and break free from our bondage to sin. In Him, you can find the power to change. Are you willing to change? If so, take a moment to pray and confess your sexual sin to the Lord. Then find or purchase some Wite-Out™ (liquid paper) and cover up all the bad grades on your report card.

7. What adjustments do you need to make in the way you think about sex and sexuality and in your sexual conduct? On your journal page, write down how the Lord has convicted you to change, and ask Him for the power to help you do so.

I'M GOING WISE

Use this page to journal. Write down what you're learning. Record your thoughts, comments, favorite verse, quotes, or questions. Compose a prayer, letter, or poem. Jot down notes from your small-group session. Draw, doodle, or diagram. Be creative. We've provided this space so you can process and apply the book whichever way is best for you.

Remember: You'll find videos, a forum, and many other resources to help you learn how to walk wisely on the GirlsGoneWise.com website. And you can follow Girls Gone Wise on Facebook (facebook.com/girlsgone-wise) and Twitter (twitter.com/girlsgonewise) too.

BOUNDARIES

Your Hedges and Precautions

Girl-Gone-**WILD**	Girl-Gone-**WISE**
Leaves Herself Susceptible	Safeguards Herself

". . . in the twilight,
in the evening,
at the time of night
and darkness."
(Proverbs 7:9)

She foresees danger
and takes precautions.
(Proverbs 22:3)

Read pages 151–166 in the **Girls Gone Wise** book.

THE MAIN POINT

A Wise Thing takes precautions in relationships. She sets up hedges to safeguard herself. In a figurative sense, the word *hedge* refers to a protective strategy that lessens the risk of something negative happening. A hedge is a personal rule that minimizes my exposure to an unwanted sexual risk. For example, "I will not go out for lunch with a male coworker alone." A hedge is a boundary that keeps me safe. It helps me protect my own sexual purity as well as the sexual purity of the men around me. It's a strategy whereby I lessen the opportunity for sin. A Wild Thing doesn't have good boundaries. She plunges ahead with reckless confidence. She scoffs at the danger, believing she's in control of the situation. She doesn't believe that she's vulnerable ("It won't happen to me!") or that the danger is substantial ("It won't hurt! What harm could it do?"). So she doesn't put up hedges and precautions to protect herself in relationships—and often ends up crashing and burning as a result.

1. Explain what a "hedge" is and what it does.

_____

_____

2. Describe a time when you (or a friend) ignored a potential danger and ended up getting into trouble because of your (or her) lack of caution.

_____

_____

3. Identify the attitude characteristic of those who fail to establish (or fail to honor) hedges.

_____

_____

4. Have you ever used any of the following rationalizations for putting yourself in a position where you are more vulnerable to sin? (Check all that apply.)

☐ "I've got everything under control."

☐ "It won't happen to me."

☐ "There's not much danger."

☐ "I can handle it."

☐ "I'm not doing anything wrong."

☐ "Everyone else is doing it."

☐ "I don't want to be a prude."

> *Girls Gone Wise*
>
> People fall into sin because they don't take the necessary personal precautions to avoid it. They lack discretion.
> *GGW*

Can you think of other possible rationalizations for failing to put up or observe a hedge?

_____

_____

5. Explain what this proverb means: "Like a gold ring in a pig's snout is a beautiful woman lacking discretion."

_____

_____

6. Read Proverbs 14:16. When it comes to boundaries, would you categorize yourself as "cautious" or as "reckless and careless"? Explain why.

_____

_____

7. Do you think that every Christian ought to have the exact same hedges? Why or why not?

_____

_____

8. Refer to the ten types of hedges listed on pages 156-165 in the book. Make a list of your own hedges in the space below and on your journaling page. If you prefer, you can use the "My Personal Hedges" Worksheet included in the appendix of this Companion Guide, on page 106.

_____

_____

_____

_____

_____

Use this page to journal. Write down what you're learning. Record your thoughts, comments, favorite verse, quotes, or questions. Compose a prayer, letter, or poem. Jot down notes from your small-group session. Draw, doodle, or diagram. Be creative. We've provided this space so you can process and apply the book whichever way is best for you.

Remember: You'll find videos, a forum, and many other resources to help you learn how to walk wisely on the GirlsGoneWise.com website. And you can follow Girls Gone Wise on Facebook (facebook.com/girlsgone-wise) and Twitter (twitter.com/girlsgonewise) too.

AUTHENTICITY
Your Public Versus Private Persona

Girl-Gone-**WILD** Two-Faced	Girl-Gone-**WISE** Genuine
"With bold face she says to him, 'I had to offer sacrifices, and today I have paid my vows.'" (Proverbs 7:13–14)	"She who walks in integrity walks securely." (Proverbs 10:9)

Read pages 167–175 in the **Girls Gone Wise** book.

THE MAIN POINT

The Wild Thing of Proverbs 7 was two-faced. The pious face she showed when she went to church wasn't the same brash face she showed after church, on that back lane, hidden in the shadows. A hypocrite is a person who deliberately and habitually professes to be good when she is aware that she is not. She puts on a religious face to impress but secretly behaves in a way totally at odds with the faith she professes. She's duplicitous. Her public persona doesn't match her private one. *Hypocrite* comes from the Greek word for an actor in a stage play. In ancient Greek comedies and tragedies, the actors wore masks to represent the characters they were playing. Hiding their true selves behind a mask is what hypocrites do. A hypocrite pretends to be very good or religious when she's aware she is not. She puts on an act to impress people. She play-acts at loving God. Like a fake designer handbag, she looks authentic, but she really isn't.

I. Why do women fear being "found out" for who they really are?

_____

_____

2. Are you a hypocrite? Review the following seven signs of hypocrisy to find out:

A. Contradiction

Who I am in public is different from who I am in private. What I say doesn't match what I do. I act like a good girl, but a naughty bad-girl streak percolates under the surface. I pretend to be who I am not.

Does this describe you?　☐ NO　☐ SOMEWHAT　☐ YES

B. Self-Indulgence

I love pleasure more than I love God. I expect God to do what I want but don't have any intention of doing what He wants. When I pray, I ask the Lord for things to indulge my passions. I'll even pray for something that clearly goes against Scripture.

Does this describe you?　☐ NO　☐ SOMEWHAT　☐ YES

C. Focus on Externals

I am more concerned about looking good than being good. I want other people to think I am spiritual and have high morals. I am very concerned about how I look to others and what they think about me. I cultivate my "good girl" image by drawing attention to the good things I do.

Does this describe you?　☐ NO　☐ SOMEWHAT　☐ YES

D. Partial Obedience

I am very selective about which parts of Scripture I choose to obey. I'm happy to do the things that draw attention to how "good" I am but will not obey if it feels uncomfortable or inconvenient, or if it goes against what I want to do.

Does this describe you?　☐ NO　☐ SOMEWHAT　☐ YES

E. Rationalization

I rationalize sin (e.g., "We're going to get married eventually"); I come up with all sorts of excuses and reasons to justify my disobedience. I talk myself into believing what I'm doing isn't wrong.

Does this describe you?　☐ NO　☐ SOMEWHAT　☐ YES

F. Contempt

I'm critical of others. I'm really good at spotting their failings and short-comings. I have high expectations about how "good" others should be, but I'm not willing to apply that same standard to myself. I feel smug and self-righteous when the sin of others is exposed. I am offended when anyone suggests I am wrong or I need to change.

Does this describe you?　☐ NO　☐ SOMEWHAT　☐ YES

G. Chameleon-Like Conduct

I change "color" depending on which environment I am in. If I'm at church, I'm a church girl. If I'm at a party, I'm a party girl. My behavior is dictated by my surroundings and the people I am with.

Does this describe you?　☐ NO　☐ SOMEWHAT　☐ YES

3. Read James 4:8–10. What problem(s) lies at the root of double-mindedness?

_____

_____

_____

4. What can you do to be more authentic?

_____

_____

_____

Girls GONE *Wise*

The problem is not when we fight against hypocrisy in our lives—but when we don't. All of us have a long way to go when it comes to true authenticity.

GGW

Use this page to journal. Write down what you're learning. Record your thoughts, comments, favorite verse, quotes, or questions. Compose a prayer, letter, or poem. Jot down notes from your small-group session. Draw, doodle, or diagram. Be creative. We've provided this space so you can process and apply the book whichever way is best for you.

Remember: You'll find videos, a forum, and many other resources to help you learn how to walk wisely on the GirlsGoneWise.com website. And you can follow Girls Gone Wise on Facebook (facebook.com/girlsgone-wise) and Twitter (twitter.com/girlsgonewise) too.

NEEDINESS

Who Do You Depend on to Fulfill Your Longings?

Girl-Gone-**WILD**	Girl-Gone-**WISE**
Depends on Man	Depends on God

"So now I have come
out to meet you,
to seek you eagerly,
and I have found you."

(Proverbs 7:15)

She delights in the Lord,
and He will give her
her heart's desires.

(Psalm 37:4)

Read pages 181–189 in the *Girls Gone Wise* book.

THE MAIN POINT

A Wild Thing is needy. She clings to a man like plastic wrap to
a piece of raw meat. Desperately thirsty, she attempts to squeeze
every drop of affection and attention out of him. She manipulates
and pressures him to make his entire life revolve around her.
She's obsessed about keeping him close. He can't go anywhere
without her. He can't see his buddies. He can't have interests or
commitments that might compete with him attending to her needs.
He must be available for her 24–7. Her happiness, her sense of self,
and even her well-being depend on it. Looking for love the wild way
differs substantially from looking for it the wise way. A Wise Thing
knows that no man on the face of the earth could ever fill the
God-shaped vacuum in her heart. She doesn't depend on men
for her source of love or sense of self. Instead, she delights in
the Lord, and looks to Him to meet her deepest longings.

I. What does neediness generally look like? What types of behaviors might a needy woman exhibit?

2. What are some life circumstances or experiences that might potentially contribute to a woman's sense of neediness?

3. What are some legitimate needs a needy woman might look to a man to fulfill?

Girls GONE *Wise*

Earthly romances are to the Cosmic One like sparkling reflections of light dancing on water are to the blazing sun. They are not the fiery light. They only reflect fleeting glimmers of it.

GGW

4. Have you ever clung to a relationship (or the hope of a relationship) to meet your deepest needs? Explain.

5. What's the problem with looking to men (or to "things") to meet the needs of our hearts?

6. Read Psalm 42:1–2. What analogy did David use to describe his soul's longing for God?

_____

_____

7. Think of a time when you felt that deep "Sehnsucht" soul-longing. Can you describe what it felt like or come up with an analogy, like David's?

_____

_____

8. Take an honest look at your life. To whom or what are you currently looking to meet the deep desires of your heart?

_____

_____

9. Read Jeremiah 17:5–8. How can you fight against the pull toward depending on relationships and other things to meet your needs? How can you stop trying to squeeze water out of those stale, leaky cisterns and turn instead to drink from the pure clear spring of God?

_____

_____

_____

_____

Use this page to journal. Write down what you're learning. Record your thoughts, comments, favorite verse, quotes, or questions. Compose a prayer, letter, or poem. Jot down notes from your small-group session. Draw, doodle, or diagram. Be creative. We've provided this space so you can process and apply the book whichever way is best for you.

Remember: You'll find videos, a forum, and many other resources to help you learn how to walk wisely on the GirlsGoneWise.com website. And you can follow Girls Gone Wise on Facebook (facebook.com/girlsgone-wise) and Twitter (twitter.com/girlsgonewise) too.

POSSESSIONS

How You Handle Your Money and Resources

Girl-Gone-**WILD** Indulgent	Girl-Gone-**WISE** Circumspect
"I have spread my couch with coverings, colored linens from Egyptian linen;I have perfumed my bed with myrrh, aloes, and cinnamon." (Proverbs 7:16-17)	"She opens her hand to the poor and reaches out her hands to the needy. . . . She makes bed coverings for herself." (Proverbs 31:20-22)

Read pages 191–198 in the *Girls Gone Wise* book.

THE MAIN POINT

What you do with money—or desire to do with it—can make
or break your happiness forever. A Wild Thing is obsessed with
spending her money, time, and energy on things to indulge her
own senses and pleasures, things she thinks will make her desirable
to men and enviable to women. She wants others to be impressed
and to hold her in high regard. She wants them to admire her
and hopes to charm them with all her finery. She wants to strut her
stuff, have fun, and indulge in things that will bring her immediate
gratification. The way she uses her money and resources all
boils down to the question of how it will best benefit her.
Wise Things don't settle for the things the world can offer.
They want immeasurably more than its cheap, temporary thrills.
A Wise Thing is circumspect about money and resources.
She spends them with a view to the needs of others
and the goal of furthering God's Kingdom.

I. If you had an unlimited amount of money, what would you buy? How would your lifestyle change? How would you spend your time?

_____

_____

2. How attracted are you to the "power of luxurious living"? Put a mark on the scale to indicate how attractive the thought is to you.

| | | | | | | | | | | | | | | | | | | | | | | | | | |

Luxurious living does not
appeal to me.

Luxurious living greatly
appeals to me.

3. Answer the following questionnaire by filling in the circle of the answer that best applies: **O** = Often, **S** = Sometimes, **R** = Rarely.

O   S   R

○ ○ ○ Are you a shopaholic?

○ ○ ○ Do you pursue pleasure through the purchase of material goods?

○ ○ ○ Do you buy things you don't really need or have the place to put?

○ ○ ○ Do you like to show off your possessions?

○ ○ ○ Do you try to impress or "wow" others with what you own?

○ ○ ○ Do you compare what you have to what others have?

○ ○ ○ Are you embarrassed if your possessions aren't as flashy or spectacular?

○ ○ ○ Are you envious of how much money others have or what they own?

○ ○ ○ Are designer labels important to you?

○ ○ ○ Are you reluctant to share or give?

○ ○ ○ Do you routinely spend more money than you have?

○ ○ ○ Do you have credit card debt?

○ ○ ○ Does your tax return indicate that you have failed to give generously?

○ ○ ○ Do you neglect to demonstrate concern for the poor and the needy?

○ ○ ○ Do you forget to pray about the purchases you make?

○ ○ ○ Are you reluctant to volunteer or pitch in to help?

○ ○ ○ Do you fail to think about how you can use your resources to further God's Kingdom?

4. Read Luke 16:1–15. *Girls Gone Wise* outlines 5 lessons from this passage about what your perspective toward money and resources ought to be. Refer to pages 191–192 to complete the chart below (the first one is done for you):

A lesson about:	What this means for me
1. Ownership	I'm just a "manager." I am accountable to God for how I spend and use His resources.
2.	
3.	
4.	
5.	

5. What type of behavior would you expect to see in someone who "treasures the riches of the Kingdom more than the riches of the world"?

_____

_____

6. What changes do you need to make in your attitude and behavior to begin investing yourself and your resources for eternity?

_____

_____

Use this page to journal. Write down what you're learning. Record your thoughts, comments, favorite verse, quotes, or questions. Compose a prayer, letter, or poem. Jot down notes from your small-group session. Draw, doodle, or diagram. Be creative. We've provided this space so you can process and apply the book whichever way is best for you.

Remember: You'll find videos, a forum, and many other resources to help you learn how to walk wisely on the GirlsGoneWise.com website. And you can follow Girls Gone Wise on Facebook (facebook.com/girlsgone-wise) and Twitter (twitter.com/girlsgonewise) too.

ENTITLEMENT

Your Insistence on Gratification

Girl-Gone-**WILD**	Girl-Gone-**WISE**
Demands Gratification	Forfeits Gratification

"Come, let us take our
fill of love till morning;
let us delight
ourselves with love."

(Proverbs 7:18)

She denies herself and
takes up her cross
daily and follows Jesus.

(Luke 9:23)

Read pages 195–202 in the *Girls Gone Wise* book.

THE MAIN POINT

Society promotes the idea that we are entitled to all sorts
of things, and a Girl-Gone-Wild has swallowed this idea hook, line,
and sinker. She insists on immediate gratification. She feels she has
a right to be comfortable, to be happy, to have fun, to get what she
wants, and to indulge in all sorts of pleasures. Enjoyment, comfort,
luxury, satisfaction, and ease are what she feels she deserves and
what she constantly seeks and demands. A Wild Thing focuses on
her rights rather than her responsibilities. It's all about HER and
what she deserves. A Girl-Gone-Wise, on the other hand, knows
that the highest pleasure exists in denying self and willingly bearing
the cross of Christ. She forfeits earthly gratification for the eternal
joy that God has set before her. For the sake of Jesus, "the Pearl
of Great Price," she is willing to suffer and pay the cost.

I. What are the things our culture says you deserve? Check all that apply:

☐ It tells me I deserve to get and do what I want.

☐ It tells me I deserve to feel good.

☐ It tells me I deserve to have life be easy and pain-free.

☐ It tells me I deserve to be loved.

☐ It tells me I deserve to be happy.

☐ It tells me I deserve to indulge.

Can you think of anything else it says you deserve?

2. Consider the following quote: "Enjoyment, comfort, luxury, and ease are what she feels she deserves and what she constantly seeks and demands." Put a mark on the scale to indicate how closely this description characterizes you.

It doesn't describe
me at all.

It accurately
describes me.

3. Why do you think people in our culture have an attitude of entitlement?

_____

_____

4. What's wrong with having an attitude of entitlement?

_____

_____

5. Explain what you think Scripture means when it says, "She who is self-indulgent is dead even while she lives" (I Timothy 5:6).

_____

_____

6. What's the connection between a woman's willingness to suffer and deny self and her ability to overcome sin?

_____

_____

7. How can you tell if someone is a "lover of pleasure" more than she is a "lover of God"?

_____

_____

_____

8. Is there something you know the Lord wants you to do, but you've been putting off because it seems too unpleasant or difficult? Explain.

_____

_____

_____

Girls GONE _Wise_

She forfeits earthly gratification for the eternal joy God has set before her. She sacrifices lesser joys for infinitely greater ones.
GGW

9. Write out a prayer on your journaling page, asking the Lord to help you treasure Him more and to increase your willingness to "take up your cross" and follow Him.

Use this page to journal. Write down what you're learning. Record your thoughts, comments, favorite verse, quotes, or questions. Compose a prayer, letter, or poem. Jot down notes from your small-group session. Draw, doodle, or diagram. Be creative. We've provided this space so you can process and apply the book whichever way is best for you.

Remember: You'll find videos, a forum, and many other resources to help you learn how to walk wisely on the GirlsGoneWise.com website. And you can follow Girls Gone Wise on Facebook (facebook.com/girlsgone-wise) and Twitter (twitter.com/girlsgonewise) too.

RELIABILITY

Your Faithfulness to Commitments

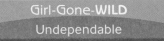

Girl-Gone-**WILD**	Girl-Gone-**WISE**
Undependable	Dependable

"For my husband is not at home; he has gone on a long journey; he took a bag of money with him; at full moon he will come home."

(Proverbs 7:19–20)

"The heart of her husband trusts in her."

(Proverbs 31:11)

Read pages 203–211 in the *Girls Gone Wise* book.

THE MAIN POINT

Wild Thing was unfaithful to her solemn marriage covenant. But breaking her promise didn't start the night she cheated on her husband. It started long before that. She broke faith when she was critical of him, when she snapped back, when she failed to forgive, when she harbored bitterness, when she withheld love, when she engaged in emotional affairs, when she read that book and watched that movie. A Wild Thing thinks the little stuff isn't all that important. But Jesus said that someone who is unfaithful in small, seemingly trivial commitments will also be unfaithful in big commitments. Faithfulness means that I do what I say I'm going to do and what our agreement obligates me to do—even when it's difficult for me. God sets the standard for reliability in the way He remains true to the Covenant. A Wise Thing strives to be as faithful to her word as God is to His.

1. What is a covenant?

_____

_____

2. Read Deuteronomy 23:21–23. Why is it important for us to be faithful to covenants?

_____

_____

3. Why is unfaithfulness to the covenant of marriage particularly reprehensible to the Lord?

_____

_____

4. To profane is to treat with irreverence or contempt, to fail to uphold as holy. Which of the following behaviors profane marriage? Check all that apply.

☐ Having an affair

☐ Flirting or messing around

☐ Watching movies that glamorize infidelity

☐ Speaking negatively about marriage

☐ Failing to honor/respect my husband

☐ Thinking I will only keep my vow if my husband keeps his

☐ Imagining an affair

☐ Reading magazines that exalt sex outside of marriage

☐ Telling or listening to off-color sexual jokes

☐ Thinking premarital sex is no big deal

☐ Thinking divorce is no big deal

☐ Failing to encourage a friend to remain faithful to her marriage vows

Girls GONE *Wise*

The covenant-keeping nature of God is the foundation for faithfulness within human relationships . . . He wants us to be as reliable to our commitments as He is to His.

GGW

5. Do you esteem and honor the covenant of marriage as much as God does? List some ways you have been guilty of profaning marriage (yours or other people's).

_____

_____

6. Describe a time when you said you would do something and then didn't do it.

_____

_____

7. Put a mark on the scale to indicate how reliable you are in "little things."

I am unreliable.   I am completely reliable.

8. Why does being reliable in "little things" matter?

_____

_____

9. In what "little thing" do you need to work at increasing your reliability?

_____

_____

Take a moment to pray and thank the Lord that He is reliable even when you are not. Confess the ways you have failed. Thank Him for His forgiveness and grace. Ask Him to transform your character so that your faithfulness to others may become more and more like His faithfulness to you.

Use this page to journal. Write down what you're learning. Record your thoughts, comments, favorite verse, quotes, or questions. Compose a prayer, letter, or poem. Jot down notes from your small-group session. Draw, doodle, or diagram. Be creative. We've provided this space so you can process and apply the book whichever way is best for you.

Remember: You'll find videos, a forum, and many other resources to help you learn how to walk wisely on the GirlsGoneWise.com website. And you can follow Girls Gone Wise on Facebook (facebook.com/girlsgone-wise) and Twitter (twitter.com/girlsgonewise) too.

SPEECH

Your Speech Habits

Girl-Gone-**WILD**	Girl-Gone-**WISE**
Excessive, Duplicitous, Manipulative	Restrained, Sincere, Without Guile

"With much seductive speech
she persuades him;
with her smooth talk
she compels him."

(Proverbs 7:21)

She keeps her tongue
from evil and her lips
from speaking guile.

(I Peter 3:10)

Read pages 213–220 in the *Girls Gone Wise* book.

THE MAIN POINT

When her provocative appearance, body language, kiss,
and scintillating invitation weren't enough, the Wild Thing of
Proverbs 7 pulled out her last and most powerful weapon—her
verbal arsenal. She talked, sweet-talked, pleaded, and persuaded
until she wore down the young man's last bit of resistance and got
her way. Women are generally more adept at using language in
interpersonal communication. They're better than men at discerning
emotions, reading body language, interpreting nonverbal cues,
and expressing thoughts, impressions, and feelings. A woman
will often use this to her advantage. She'll talk and talk until
the guy gets overwhelmed, befuddled, or frustrated and agrees
with her or gives in to her demands. A Girl-Gone-Wild talks
a lot. And she's duplicitous and manipulative with her words.
But restrained, sincere, non-manipulative, gracious
speech is the mark of a Girl-Gone-Wise.

I. According to the Bible, what's the problem with talking excessively?

_____

_____

2. Describe a situation in which excessive speech has gotten you into trouble.

_____

_____

3. What are the emotions or circumstances that typically trigger you to say too much?

_____

_____

_____

4. In your own words, explain what is meant by the phrase "sweet talk" (or "smooth talker").

_____

_____

_____

> Like an angler baits a hook to catch a fish, so a guileful woman hangs her words to bait a man. She conceals her true thoughts and intentions while trying to hook him into doing what she wants.
>
> _GGW_

5. What's wrong with using "sweet talk" or flattery to get what you want?

_____

_____

6. Do you conceal your true thoughts and intentions while trying to hook a guy into doing what you want? Why do you (and/or other women) use this tactic?

_____

_____

7. How can using words to beguile, control, and manipulate a man backfire on a woman? How has it backfired on you?

_____

_____

8. Rank the following three faulty types of speech from #1 to #3, indicating which is the biggest (1) to the smallest (3) problem for you:

_____ Excessive (Nagging)

_____ Duplicitous (Baiting)

_____ Manipulative (Controlling)

9. According to Proverbs 8:6–11, what are some characteristics of wise speech? Make a list below:

_____

_____

_____

_____

_____

 Ask the Lord to help you mind your mouth and be wise and not wild in the way you talk. To help you, I've provided a special "Conversation Peace" quiz you can download at girlsgonewise.com/ggw.

Use this page to journal. Write down what you're learning. Record your thoughts, comments, favorite verse, quotes, or questions. Compose a prayer, letter, or poem. Jot down notes from your small-group session. Draw, doodle, or diagram. Be creative. We've provided this space so you can process and apply the book whichever way is best for you.

Remember: You'll find videos, a forum, and many other resources to help you learn how to walk wisely on the GirlsGoneWise.com website. And you can follow Girls Gone Wise on Facebook (facebook.com/girlsgone-wise) and Twitter (twitter.com/girlsgonewise) too.

INFLUENCE

Your Impact on Others and Their Impact on You

Girl-Gone-**WILD** Negative Influence	Girl-Gone-**WISE** Positive Influence
"She persuades him. . . . She compels him. All at once he follows her, as an ox goes to the slaughter. . . . He does not know that it will cost him his life." (Proverbs 7:21–23)	"Whoever walks with the wise becomes wise, but the companion of fools will suffer harm." (Proverbs 13:20)

Read pages 221–229 in the **Girls Gone Wise** book.

THE MAIN POINT

Influence is the power to sway. It's the power somebody has
to affect another person's thinking or actions. The Wild Thing
of Proverbs 7 was the negative influence that compelled the young
man to sin. That's not to say he wasn't responsible for his behavior.
He was just as guilty as she was. But she was the bad influence—
the fatal attraction—that pulled him away from walking God's way.
Negative influence is very powerful. Not only does the Bible want
us to stop being a negative influence on others, it also wants us to
avoid people who might exert a negative influence on us. A Wise
Thing heeds the age-old warning that "Bad company corrupts good
morals." She does not take on just anybody as a close friend. She
takes a look at the person's character and chooses her confidants
carefully. She knows that if she constantly and exclusively hangs out
with people who don't love the Lord, chances are they'll have
a greater influence on her than she will have on them.

I. In your own words, define "influence."

_____

_____

2. Do you agree that "Bad company ruins good morals"? Why or why not?

_____

_____

3. Describe a time when you watched a friend get messed up due to associating with bad company.

_____

_____

4. Read I Corinthians 5:9–11. Why do you think Paul told his friends to avoid hanging out with hypocrites?

_____

_____

_____

Girls GONE *Wise*

Negative influence is very powerful. Not only does the Bible want us to stop being a negative influence on others, but it also wants us to avoid people who might exert a negative influence on us.

GGW

5. What are some common reasons or rationalizations for getting involved with a person who could potentially be a bad influence? Have you ever used any of these reasons/rationalizations?

_____

_____

_____

6. On the chart below, list some signs that would indicate that someone is exerting a positive influence and some signs that would indicate that his or her influence is negative.

Signs of positive influence	Signs of negative influence

7. How can a woman exert a godly influence on a man without reverting to nagging, manipulation, or control?

_____

_____

8. There's a saying that goes, "Tell me your friends, and I'll tell you who you are." What do the behavior and character of your friends say about you?

_____

_____

9. Do you need to make some adjustments in the company you keep? Why or why not?

_____

_____

Use this page to journal. Write down what you're learning. Record your thoughts, comments, favorite verse, quotes, or questions. Compose a prayer, letter, or poem. Jot down notes from your small-group session. Draw, doodle, or diagram. Be creative. We've provided this space so you can process and apply the book whichever way is best for you.

Remember: You'll find videos, a forum, and many other resources to help you learn how to walk wisely on the GirlsGoneWise.com website. And you can follow Girls Gone Wise on Facebook (facebook.com/girlsgone-wise) and Twitter (twitter.com/girlsgonewise) too.

SUSTAINABILITY

Your Ability to Nurture and Sustain a Relationship

Girl-Gone-**WILD**	Girl-Gone-**WISE**
Relationships Deteriorate	Relationships Grow

"For many a victim
has she laid low,
and all her slain
are a mighty throng."

(Proverbs 7:26)

"The wisest of women
builds her house,
but folly with her own
hands tears it down."

(Proverbs 14:1)

Read pages 231–239 in the *Girls Gone Wise* book.

THE MAIN POINT

The wild behavior of the woman in our narrative interfered
with her ability to make relationships work. She had a series of
men in her life and in her bed. Her heart was like a revolving door—
one guy after another passed through. Perhaps one or two of them
stayed longer, but inevitably each relationship broke down. She was
unable to sustain it long-term. And her marriage was headed toward
the same fate. A Wild Thing gives her heart and affections away
far too quickly and to the wrong kind of man. Sadly, each failure
magnifies the chance of failing again. Another pattern that's evident
in a Wild Thing is her lack of respect. Not only does she disrespect
God's pattern for relationships, she also disrespects men.
She's a male basher. She's not a builder; she's a destroyer. Wise
Things nurture and grow their relationships. Wild Things
behave to destroy them. They tragically cripple and
sabotage the very thing they hope to gain.

1. Why do you think women get caught in the revolving door of failed relationships?

2. Do you think a Christian woman's disregard for God's ways is mostly intentional or unintentional?

3. What life circumstances and experiences might make it more difficult for a woman to respect God's pattern and approach to male-female relationships?

If you want a lasting, fulfilling relationship, you will go about it in God's way. You will respect Him.
GGW

4. If a woman has had difficult life experiences, feels wounded and needy, and has gone through several failed relationships, what do you think she needs in order to be willing and able to do things God's way?

5. What are some ways women and our culture disrespect men?

6. Describe a time when you've demonstrated a lack of respect toward men or noticed a disrespectful attitude in your spirit.

_____

_____

7. How is disrespect for men a sign of disrespect for God?

_____

_____

8. Read Proverbs 14:1. What are you foolishly doing to tear your own house down?

_____

_____

9. What do you need to do to build rather than destroy your relationship?

_____

_____

If you've been caught in the door of revolving relationships, ask the Lord to help you understand why. Do you need Him to heal an old wound? Do you need to turn to Him rather than men for validation? Are you failing to respect God's way of doing things? Seek out wise counsel and get prayer to help you break free of the revolving-door pattern.

Use this page to journal. Write down what you're learning. Record your thoughts, comments, favorite verse, quotes, or questions. Compose a prayer, letter, or poem. Jot down notes from your small-group session. Draw, doodle, or diagram. Be creative. We've provided this space so you can process and apply the book whichever way is best for you.

Remember: You'll find videos, a forum, and many other resources to help you learn how to walk wisely on the GirlsGoneWise.com website. And you can follow Girls Gone Wise on Facebook (facebook.com/girlsgone-wise) and Twitter (twitter.com/girlsgonewise) too.

TEACHABILITY

Your Willingness to Be Corrected and Instructed

Girl-Gone-**WILD**	Girl-Gone-**WISE**
Scornful	Teachable

"Woe to her who is
rebellious and defiled. . . .
She listens to no voice;
she accepts no correction.
She does not trust in
the LORD; she does not
draw near to her God."

(Zephaniah 3:1–2)

"The ear that listens
to life-giving reproof
will dwell among
the wise."

(Proverbs 15:31)

Read pages 241–252 in the ***Girls Gone Wise*** book.

THE MAIN POINT

Everyone loves going to a dinner party where the food is delectable, the company is enjoyable, and the entertainment is first-class. We're all invited to attend two very different banquets: Lady Wise is calling for guests to come and dine at her table; Lady Wild is also extending an invitation. And you have to make a choice about which party you're going to attend. Both of the main characters in our story—the naïve young man and the wily seductress who caused his downfall—turned down wisdom's invitation. They exemplify the types of individuals who choose to dine with Lady Wild instead: simple people, fools, and scoffers. All of Lady Wild's guests are characterized by various levels of resistance to learning and hostility to doing things God's way.

A Wild Thing doesn't think she needs input, but a Wise Thing is teachable. She welcomes the correction and training that are part of the delicious banquet served at the table of Lady Wise.

I. Identify the trait that characterizes each type of Wild Thing. (See *GGW*, page 249.)

Simple Sally: _____

Foolish Fran: _____

Scoffing Sue: _____

2. What danger exists for those who don't make an effort to learn the ways of the Lord and for those who think they've got it all figured out?

_____

_____

3. Think of times when you (or your girlfriends) reached a crisis point that caused you (or them) to turn from foolishness to wisdom. What were some of the crises that became catalysts for change?

_____

_____

4. Why do you think it often takes a crisis to get a foolish woman to turn from her sin?

_____

_____

5. Which profile best describes your approach to relationships up to this point?

☐ Simple Sally   ☐ Foolish Fran   ☐ Scoffing Sue   ☐ Lady Wise

Explain why.

_____

_____

_____

6. According to the profile you chose, what do you need in order to continue changing from wild to wise?

_____

_____

7. What is meant by the phrase "The fear of the Lord is the beginning of wisdom"?

_____

_____

_____

8. If "fear of the Lord" is wisdom's most essential element, how will you know if you are increasing in wisdom?

_____

_____

_____

Girls GONE *Wise*

A personification of the trait of wisdom, Lady Wise invites you to her feast. Above the din and bustle of daily life, she cries out and summons you to sit down at her table.

GGW

9. Lady Wild and Lady Wise both invite you to their tables. Whose invitation sounds more attractive to you, and why?

_____

_____

10. Are you committed to dining at the table of Lady Wise? If so, write out a prayer of commitment on your journaling page.

Use this page to journal. Write down what you're learning. Record your thoughts, comments, favorite verse, quotes, or questions. Compose a prayer, letter, or poem. Jot down notes from your small-group session. Draw, doodle, or diagram. Be creative. We've provided this space so you can process and apply the book whichever way is best for you.

Remember: You'll find videos, a forum, and many other resources to help you learn how to walk wisely on the GirlsGoneWise.com website. And you can follow Girls Gone Wise on Facebook (facebook.com/girlsgone-wise) and Twitter (twitter.com/girlsgonewise) too.

WILD TO WISE

That Most Beautiful Woman in the World

"The beginning of wisdom is this: Get wisdom,
and whatever you get, get insight.
Prize her highly, and she will exalt you;
she will honor you if you embrace her.
She will place on your head a graceful garland;
she will bestow on you a beautiful crown."

(Proverbs 4:7–9)

Read pages 253–260 in the **Girls Gone Wise** book.

THE MAIN POINT

We've come to the end of the *Girls Gone Wise* book. I hope you've enjoyed reading and studying along. And I hope that you've learned that this story in Proverbs 7 isn't just the story of a Wild Thing who cheated on her husband. It's a story that demonstrates that there's a measure of wildness in each of us. You have wild tendencies—and so do I. The Proverbs 7 story didn't end well. The choices that Wild Thing made didn't lead to the happily-ever-after ending she had hoped for. Her behavior prevented her from experiencing a life of wholeness and freedom. She ended up with a fractured heart, a fractured spirit, and fractured relationships—with men, and even more tragically, with the Lord. The thing I love about the Bible, and the thing that I want to stress as we finish up our time together, is that Jesus can take the most messed-up storyline and redeem it. No matter how badly we've messed up, He pours out His forgiveness and grace. He offers us His power to change. He wants us to experience the alternate ending, the happily-ever-after one we all yearn for. He enables us to change from wild to wise and to become that most beautiful woman in the world.

1. Have you ever felt, like the Samaritan Woman, that no matter how hard you try to fill your bucket, it remains empty?

_____

_____

2. Describe how you think the Samaritan Woman felt when she met Jesus and He forgave all her sin and filled her bucket to the brim with living water.

_____

_____

3. Read Isaiah 55:1–3, 6–7 at the bottom of page 257. Have you accepted Christ's invitation and experienced His "abundant pardon" for your sin? Do you truly believe He forgives and satisfies the soul-thirst of all who seek Him? Explain.

_____

_____

4. How would an appreciation for Christ's abundant grace keep you from focusing on your shortcomings and encourage you to keep working at becoming less wild and more wise?

_____

_____

5. To refresh your memory about areas you need to work on, complete the "Wild or Wise? 20 Points of Contrast" quiz on page 104.

6. What are the top three Points of Contrast you struggle with, that you would like the Lord to help you change?

1. _____

2. _____

3. _____

7. Which insight from this book did you find the most valuable?

_____

_____

8. How do you plan to support the "quiet counterrevolution" of women committed to living according to God's design? Are there some friends with whom you can share the Girls Gone Wise message? Is there a younger woman you can begin to disciple?

_____

_____

_____

_____

_____

Any woman can become a Wise Thing. Any woman can become that most beautiful woman in the world. The choice is yours. Will it be you?
GGW

9. Why is no woman quite as beautiful as a Girl-Gone-Wise?

_____

_____

Hey, Girlfriend,

Has *Girls Gone Wise* made a difference in your life? If this study has been meaningful to you, would you take a few moments to email or write me a letter and share how God has used it to help you change from wild to wise? Here are some things you might want to include:

- Your testimony of turning from wild to wise.
- Specific ways you have lived as a Girl-Gone-Wild.
- Consequences you have experienced as a result of living that way.
- Specific truths you have learned about how to live as a Girl-Gone-Wise.
- Changes that have taken place in your life as a result.
- How God used this study in your small group, or in the life of a friend.

You can email me at DearMary@girlsgonewise.com or send a letter snail mail via my publisher:

Mary Kassian
Girls Gone Wise
c/o Moody Publishers
820 North La Salle Blvd.
Chicago, IL 60610

Thanks for taking the time to share your story. It will be a great encouragement to me—and it may influence someone who needs to hear how God has been faithful to a sister facing similar issues or circumstances. May God bless you as you continue to grow and do your best to walk on His path.

Gratefully,

Mary

Mary Kassian
Girls Gone Wise
girlsgonewise.com

Dear Mary,

_____

_____

_____

_____

_____

_____

_____

_____

_____

_____

_____

_____

_____

_____

_____

_____

_____

_____

_____

_____

_____

_____

Please indicate:

"Mary, you have my permission to share my story with others . . .

☐ with my first name,   ☐ using a different name, or,

☐ changing details that could reveal my identity."

The Wild Thing of Proverbs 7

20 POINTS OF CONTRAST

1. **Heart**	Her feet go down to death; her steps follow the path to Sheol; she does not ponder the path of life.	What Holds First Place in Her Affections	Wild: Christ Is Peripheral Wise: Christ Is Central
2. **Counsel**	She does not ponder the path of life; her ways wander, and she does not know it.	Where She Gets Her Instruction	Wild: World-Instructed Wise: Word-Instructed
3. **Approach**	A woman meets him . . . wily of heart.	Who Directs Her Love Story	Wild: Self-Manipulated Wise: God-Orchestrated
4. **Attitude**	She is loud and wayward.	Her Prevailing Disposition	Wild: Clamorous and Defiant Wise: Gentle, Calm, Amenable
5. **Habits**	Her feet do not stay at home; now in the street, now in the market, and at every corner.	Her Priorities and Routines	Wild: Self-Indulgent Wise: Self-Disciplined
6. **Focus**	She lies in wait.	What Commands Her Attention	Wild: Getting Wise: Giving
7. **Appearance**	She's dressed as a prostitute.	How She Adorns Herself	Wild: Unbecoming, Indecent, Excessive Wise: Becoming, Decent, Moderate
8. **Body Language**	She's graceful and of deadly charms.	Her Nonverbal Behavior	Wild: Suggestive Wise: Demure
9. **Roles**	She seizes him. He follows her.	Her Pattern of Interaction	Wild: Inclined to Dominate Wise: Inclined to Follow
10. **Sexual Conduct**	She kisses him.	Her Sexual Behavior	Wild: Impure and Dishonorable Wise: Pure and Honorable

11. Boundaries	She meets him in the twilight, in the evening, at the time of night and darkness.	Her Hedges and Precautions	Wild: Leaves Herself Susceptible Wise: Safeguards Herself
12. Authenticity	And with bold face she says to him, "I had to offer sacrifices, and today I have paid my vows."	Her Public Versus Private Persona	Wild: Two-Faced Wise: Genuine
13. Neediness	"So now I have come out to meet you, to seek you eagerly."	Who She Depends on to Fulfill Her Longings	Wild: Depends on Man Wise: Depends on God
14. Possessions	"I have spread my couch with coverings, colored linens from Egyptian linen."	How She Handles Her Money and Resources	Wild: Indulgent Wise: Circumspect
15. Entitlement	"Come, let us take our fill of love; let us delight ourselves with love."	Her Insistence on Gratification	Wild: Demands Gratification Wise: Forfeits Gratification
16. Reliability	"For my husband is not at home; he has gone on a long journey."	Her Faithfulness to Commitments	Wild: Undependable Wise: Dependable
17. Speech	With much seductive speech, with her smooth talk . . .	Her Speech Habits	Wild: Excessive, Duplicitous, Manipulative Wise: Restrained, Sincere, Without Guile
18. Influence	She persuades him. She compels him.	Her Impact on Others and Their Impact on Her	Wild: Negative Influence Wise: Positive Influence
19. Sustainability	Many a victim she laid low, all her slain are a mighty throng.	Her Ability to Nurture and Sustain a Relationship	Wild: Relationships Deteriorate Wise: Relationships Grow
20. Teachability	She listens to no voice; she accepts no correction.	Her Willingness to be Corrected and Instructed	Wild: Scornful Wise: Teachable

My Personal Hedges
Worksheet

A hedge is a personal rule that minimizes a woman's exposure to an unwanted sexual risk. It's a boundary that helps her protect her own sexual purity as well as the sexual purity of the men around her. It's a strategy whereby she seeks to honor God and lessen the opportunity for sin.

This worksheet is to help you establish what your personal hedges are. Cross out the suggestions for hedges that don't apply to you or ones you don't like or don't want. There's also space provided to write in any additional or alternate hedges you might want to establish for yourself. Remember, a hedge only works if you are committed to honoring that boundary. Your hedges may differ from other girls. That's okay. This is *your* list. It should reflect the hedges you are committed to.

I. Location Hedges: unhealthy versus healthy environments

A Girl-Gone-Wise avoids unhealthy environments.

- ☐ I will not go to bars, lounges, or clubs.

- ☐ I will not go to strip shows or lewd bachelorette parties.

- ☐ I will not go to any parties that involve drinking, drugs, or sex.

- ☐ I will not go to X-rated movies.

- ☐ I will not go to restaurants that encourage servers to dress and act provocatively.

- ☐ I will not go to comedy clubs that feature foul language and crude sexual humor.

- ☐ If I find myself in an unhealthy environment, I will quickly leave.

_____

_____

_____

_____

2. **Pairing** Hedges: dual versus group interaction

A Girl-Gone-Wise avoids inappropriately pairing herself with men.

- ☐ I will interact with men in groups rather than one-on-one situations.

- ☐ I will not meet up, dine, or travel alone with a man if one of us is married.

- ☐ I will try to avoid being paired with men in work projects, school assignments, or volunteer work. If pairing up is unavoidable, I will strengthen and emphasize other hedges to compensate for this.

- ☐ As an unmarried woman, I will not pair off with an unmarried man (one-on-one) until I have had ample opportunity to get to know him in a group context.

_____

_____

_____

_____

3. **Seclusion** Hedges: private versus public venues

A Girl-Gone-Wise avoids being in private, secluded places with men.

- ☐ I will not be alone with a man in a bedroom, apartment, house, hotel room, cabin, or any other place cut-off from public view.

- ☐ I will interact with men in places where other people in the vicinity can potentially observe our interaction.

- ☐ If I am meeting alone with a man in a business context, I will ensure to keep the door of the room open or to meet in a room with glass walls or windows.

- ☐ If I am meeting with a man by webcam (e.g., Skype), I will observe these same precautions.

_____

_____

_____

_____

4. **Communication** Hedges: inscrutable versus open interaction

A Girl-Gone-Wise avoids secret communication with men.

☐ I will keep my electronic communication clean and pure, and free of all sexual flirtation, innuendo, and other sexual content.

☐ I will copy my spouse, the recipient's spouse, or other recipients if emails contain interaction of a personal nature.

☐ I will not communicate anything verbally or in writing that I would be hesitant to share with my spouse or a godly mentor.

☐ If I receive an inappropriate message, I will forward the message to my spouse or godly mentor and copy him or her on my response.

_____

_____

_____

_____

5. **Contact** Hedges: copious versus controlled contact

A Girl-Gone-Wise controls the frequency and amount of contact with men.

☐ I will not initiate or reciprocate inappropriate contact with a man if one of us is married.

☐ If I feel "pulled" toward an adulterous relationship, I will immediately pull back and break off or minimize contact with him.

☐ Before I am married, I will resist the pull to spend time with a guy as though I were married to him. I will resist the pull to be constantly together just as I resist the pull toward sexual intimacy. (You may want to limit the number of times you are together each week, based on what's appropriate for your age and circumstance.)

☐ I will not monopolize a guy's time or attention.

☐ I will not clamor for a guy's attention by sending him excessive texts or messages.

☐ I will not needlessly interrupt and distract him by calling and texting him when he is busy.

☐ I will not allow a guy to monopolize my time or attention.

☐ I will not neglect my obligations, responsibilities, or ministry opportunities.

☐ I will encourage him to attend to his obligations, responsibilities, and ministry opportunities.

☐ I will not neglect my family relationships or other friendships.

☐ I will encourage him not to neglect his family relationships or other friendships.

_____

_____

_____

_____

6. **Curfew Hedges: cover-of-night versus light-of-day parameters**

   A Girl-Gone-Wise abides by curfew and nighttime boundaries.

   ☐ I will keep the lights on when I am in a room with a man I am not married to.

   ☐ I will not sleep over at a man's apartment or house.

   ☐ I will be home before . . . (11 p.m., midnight, 1 a.m., etc.)

   ☐ I will turn off my computer by . . . (10 p.m., 11 p.m., midnight, 1 a.m., etc.)

   ☐ I will not send texts after . . . (9 p.m., 10 p.m., etc.)

   ☐ I will get to bed by . . . (10 p.m., 11 p.m., midnight, 1 a.m., etc.)

   _____

   _____

   _____

   _____

7. **Disclosure Hedges: deep versus superficial disclosure**

   A Girl-Gone-Wise doesn't inappropriately confide in men.

   ☐ I will not disclose my inner self to a man when it is inappropriate to do so, or (in the case of unmarried individuals) premature to do so.

☐ If I feel an emotional pull toward an illicit relationship, I will confess that pull to a trusted godly friend or mentor, so she can pray for me and hold me accountable to maintain boundaries.

☐ Unless there is another person present, I will not allow a man to confide in me about difficulties he is having with his wife.

☐ I will not offer a man the emotional support he ought to receive from his wife.

(The following hedges are specific to married women.)

☐ I will only express admiration or compliments for a man in a group setting, where others can hear my remarks.

☐ Unless there is another person present, I will keep conversations with men on a superficial level.

☐ If I need to talk about struggles in my marriage, I will seek out a godly female friend or mentor and will not speak of them to another man.

☐ I will not seek from another man the emotional support I ought to receive from my husband.

☐ If I feel an emotional connection with a man that tempts me to cross any boundaries, I will immediately pull back and tighten and strengthen the boundaries.

_____

_____

_____

_____

8. **Encroachment** Hedges: wide-open versus guarded demeanor

A Girl-Gone-Wise doesn't leave herself open and unguarded.

☐ I will not sit or stand too close to men.

☐ I will not provocatively position my body.

☐ I will not tease men with provocative body language.

☐ I will not wear revealing clothing.

☐ I will physically distance myself from men who encroach on my personal space.

☐ I will distance myself from men who fail to respect me or my standards for purity.

_____

_____

_____

_____

9. **Touching Hedges: improper versus proper physical contact**

A Girl-Gone-Wise maintains strict boundaries of physical contact with men (friend/boyfriend/fiancé).

☐ I will restrict my physical contact with men to socially appropriate forms of greeting such as a handshake, hug (from the shoulders up), or in the case of close friends or family, a peck on the cheek.

☐ I will not allow a man to touch parts of my body other than my hands, arms, upper back, and shoulders.

☐ I will dress modestly and will always keep all of my clothes on when I'm with a man.

☐ I will not allow a man to touch parts of my body that I have covered with clothing. (Note that in Ezekiel 23:21 the Lord identifies pressing or touching breasts as lewd conduct.)

☐ I will not unbutton or unfasten articles of clothing and expose my nakedness to a man.

☐ I will not allow a man to look at or touch my private parts.

☐ I will not allow a man to kiss me anywhere except on the face and lips.

☐ I will not look at or touch a man's private parts.

☐ I will not lie down on a couch or bed with a man.

☐ I will not lie under or on top of a man, or position myself against him in any way that mimics the posture of sexual intercourse.

☐ I will only hold hands, hug, and kiss (from the shoulders up.)

☐ I will save my first kiss for marriage. (*Reminder: This is just one of many options for potential hedges.*)

☐ I will not touch a man in private in any way that we would not touch in public.

_____

_____

_____

_____

10. **Covenant** Hedges: dishonoring versus honoring marital unions

A Girl-Gone-Wise does everything she can to honor and affirm marriage covenants.

☐ I will always wear my wedding ring.

☐ I will reinforce the fact that I am "one" with my husband by mentioning him and by using inclusive words like "we," "us," and "our" when I talk about my personal life.

☐ I will affirm and support the marriages of others by inquiring about their spouses and acknowledging them in verbal and written conversation.

☐ I will try to get to know the wives of men I interact with, and whenever possible, relate to the husband and wife together, as a couple.

☐ I will never say or do anything to threaten or diminish the sanctity of marriage.

_____

_____

_____

_____

Other: _____

_____

_____

_____

Girls Gone Wise

Wild or Wise?
20 Points of Contrast

For each point of contrast, circle the number on the scale that best describes you.

1. **Heart**—What holds first place in my affections:

0	1	2	3	4	5

Christ Is Peripheral — Christ Is Central

2. **Counsel**—Where I get my instruction:

0	1	2	3	4	5

World-Instructed — Word-Instructed

3. **Approach**—Who directs my love story:

0	1	2	3	4	5

Self-Manipulated — God-Orchestrated

4. **Attitude**—My prevailing disposition:

0	1	2	3	4	5

Clamorous and Defiant — Gentle, Calm, Amenable

5. **Habits**—My priorities and routines:

0	1	2	3	4	5

Self-Indulgent — Self-Disciplined

6. **Focus**—What commands my attention:

0	1	2	3	4	5

Getting — Giving

7. **Appearance**—How I adorn myself:

0	1	2	3	4	5

Unbecoming, Indecent, Excessive — Becoming, Decent, Moderate

8. **Body Language**—My nonverbal behavior:

0	1	2	3	4	5

Suggestive   Demure

9. **Roles**—My pattern of interaction:

0	1	2	3	4	5

Inclined to Dominate   Inclined to Follow

10. **Sexuality**—My sexual behavior:

0	1	2	3	4	5

Impure and Dishonorable   Pure and Honorable

11. **Boundaries**—My hedges and precautions:

0	1	2	3	4	5

Leave Myself Susceptible   Safeguard Myself

12. **Authenticity**—My public versus private persona:

0	1	2	3	4	5

Two-Faced   Genuine

13. **Neediness**—Who I depend on to fulfill my longings:

0	1	2	3	4	5

Depend on Man   Depend on God

14. **Possessions**—How I manage my resources:

0	1	2	3	4	5

Indulgent   Circumspect

15. **Entitlement**—My insistence on gratification:

0	1	2	3	4	5

Demand Gratification   Forfeit Gratification

16. **Reliability**—My faithfulness to commitments:

0	1	2	3	4	5

Undependable   Dependable

17. **Speech**—My speech habits:

0	1	2	3	4	5

Excessive, Duplicitous, Manipulative   Restrained, Sincere, Without Guile

18. **Influence**—My impact on others and their impact on me:

0	1	2	3	4	5

Negative Influence   Positive Influence

19. **Sustainability**—My ability to nurture and sustain relationships:

0	1	2	3	4	5

Relationships Deteriorate   Relationships Grow

20. **Teachability**—My willingness to be corrected:

0	1	2	3	4	5

Scornful   Teachable

If you like, you can add up your score to a possible 100. _____

Are you: ☐ more wise or ☐ more wild?

In which three areas would you like the Lord to help you have more smarts?

_____

_____

_____

**Remember to carefully consider how you walk,
so that you might increase in wisdom!**

MORE RESOURCES ...

**Girls Gone Wise
Paperback**

**Girls Gone Wise
DVD**

**Girls Gone Wise
Group Study Kit**

MoodyPublishers.com | GirlsGoneWise.com

... FOR GIRLS GONE WISE

You'll find videos, a forum, and many other resources to help you learn how to walk wisely on the GirlsGoneWise.com website. And make sure to follow *Girls Gone Wise* on Facebook (facebook.com/girlgonewise) and Twitter (twitter.com/girlsgonewise) too!

Also available, *Girls Gone Wise* gear!
Get the bag, mug, and buttons.